Normal Isn't a Compliment

Kaitlyn Tiara

BookLeaf
Publishing

India | USA | UK

Normal Isn't a Compliment © 2022

Kaitlyn Tiara

All rights reserved.

No part of this publication may be reproduced, stored in a retrieval system, or transmitted, in any form or by any means, electronic, mechanical, photocopying, recording or otherwise, without the prior written permission of the presenters.

Kaitlyn Tiara asserts the moral right to be identified as the author of this work.

Presentation by *BookLeaf Publishing*

Web: www.bookleafpub.com

E-mail: info@bookleafpub.com

ISBN: 9789357444521

First edition 2022

These works are dedicated to all those who have touched my life and supported my journey, whether they knew it or not.

ACKNOWLEDGEMENT

The list for whom to thank goes on for miles. I have to thank my grandparents Donita and Ballard, my parents Chelsea and Joe, and my sister Tessa for their unwavering support and the joy they bring to my life. I also owe a huge thank you to my partner, Allan, for his encouragement and inspiration. I have an array of friends who have been so impactful in my mental health journey; it would take an entire book to list and thank them all for what they've done for me, and that still wouldn't be enough.

PREFACE

Mental health is gradually becoming less taboo; however, the stigma against those living with mental illnesses is prevalent and intense. Talking openly about struggles and triumphs can reduce stigma, encourage those who need it to seek treatment, and help their loved ones learn how to provide healthy support.

Grey Days

Another grey day
where the sun cannot shine
or warm the ice in my veins
the darkness in my brain
blocks the street lights
illuminating hope
leviathans of self-loathing
escaped their cages and ran free
paralyzed by fog and lost in a daze
I don't have the energy
to chase the fading light
at the end of the cave
I'm trapped in
I'm too far away to be found
so I'll drown in my head
and wait for the fog to lift
so the sun can wrap me in self-love
and I can live in vibrant color

Hypomania

I open my eyes to the vibrant colors and
beautiful melodies of life
I drink coffee though I know I don't need it
today I have energy
motivation – usually fleeting – follows me from
task to task
I can't sit still

I call my friends to make plans
"are you free right now?"
I call my family and race through life updates
even if I've already told them
I can't be alone

I run errands
$300 on groceries for one
$1000 on fish I'll kill
$300 on a TV I don't watch
$500 on various gaming systems I won't play
Where can I go next?
I can't go home

I drive to the mountains to get lost in the beauty
then lose on the road
I cross state lines, radio too loud to think
the road and unfamiliar surroundings

keep my brain stimulated enough to be alone
but for how long?

Where do I end?

How do I know where I stop
and hypomania starts?
How many good days have I ruined
obsessing over every thought
every action
every feeling
I analyze myself to the point of extinction

I'm more than a case study
I don't have to have all the answers

Fall Rain

Wind roars through the leaves
raindrops dance on the sill of my open window
the crisp, clean smell of rain fills my lungs as I
breathe
colorful leaves fall to the ground as they're
shaken from their limbs
my coffee tastes a little better than usual
I sip and let the warm drink fill my belly as the
chilly breeze touches my body
My blankets feel a little cozier today
I snuggle in close and feel the soft fleece hug me
I can feel the plants grow as the rain falls
reaching their roots out to drink their fill
and the earth refreshes my soul
so I'll stay here
cozy in bed
and drink up my coffee and drink in the rain

Sunshine

Sunshine, steady and strong
touches the earth and gives life
plants stretch to bask in its warmth
and feel the safety of its rays
sunshine caresses my skin
warming me to my core
as I lay in the cool grass
rays of colorful heat
wrap me in serenity
I close my eyes to its comfort
and trust in its consistency

My soul floats through space
untethered
unrestricted
gliding among the brilliant, sparkling stars
passion shines vibrant colors through my mind
a supernova explosion
and now I float
freely
wildly
effortlessly
through endless, glittering space

Stardust

My soul floats through space
untethered
unrestricted
gliding amongst the brilliant, sparkling stars
passion shines vibrant colors through my mind
a supernova explosion
and now I float
freely
wildly
effortlessly
through endless, glittering space

"But You Seem So Normal"

I confide my diagnosis to another
"but you seem so normal!" they reply
their intentions were kind but their words cut
like knives
as they praise me for wearing a mask that hides
my pain
to fit into society's mold of productivity
instead of praising me for showing my colors
and advocating for myself and others

Masks

I stare at my reflection in the mirror
at pale grey eyes, dull with lack of luster
I put on my mask for the day
to hide the struggles
the instability
the impulsiveness
the lack of focus
the sadness
the numbness
the distractability
the irritability
the exhaustion
I paint myself with stability and composure
and avoid looking at anyone for too long
lest they see the pale grey eyes behind the mask

The Med Game

My psychiatrist listens to me tell my story
She asks questions and scribbles a prescription
The pharmacist asks if I have any questions
about my new medication
I say no, unsure what to ask
The medicine makes me nauseated
I wait weeks to see the effects
I monitor my body, my weight, my appetite, my
sex drive, my productivity
This medicine makes my brain feel like it's
wrapped in jell-o
I schedule a psychiatric appointment

My psychiatrist listens to me tell my story
She asks questions and scribbles a prescription
The pharmacist asks if I have any questions
about my new medication
I made a list
The medicine makes me nauseated
I wait weeks to see the effects
I monitor my body, my weight, my appetite, my
sex drive, my productivity
This medicine helps the hypomania
But the depression is so much worse
I schedule a psychiatric appointment

My psychiatrist listens to me tell my story
She asks questions and scribbles a prescription
The pharmacist asks if I have any questions
about my new medication
I ask the questions I've memorized
The medicine makes me nauseated
I wait weeks to see the effects
I monitor my body, my weight, my appetite, my
sex drive, my productivity
This medicine helps the depression be
manageable
But the anxiety is overwhelming
I schedule a psychiatric appointment

My psychiatrist listens to me tell my story
She asks questions and scribbles a prescription
The pharmacist asks if I have any questions
about my new medication
I say no, they're the same as the last one
The medicine makes me nauseated
I wait weeks to see the effects
I monitor my body, my weight, my appetite, my
sex drive, my productivity
This medicine helps me feel less anxious
I schedule a psychiatric appointment

My psychiatrist listens to me tell my story
She asks questions
We combine medicines and adjust dosages

making my personal stability cocktail
I monitor my body, my weight, my appetite, my
sex drive, my productivity
I schedule follow up appointments for every 90
days
to make sure I'm still winning the med game

Buzzing Beehive

My jaw aches
It has been clenched for hours
The ache radiates up to my brain
I want to close my eyes and rest
but my brain is a beehive someone hit with a bat
buzzing with fear and anticipation and anger
I can't make the bees be quiet
and I can't make them pause long enough to
complete a thought
I get lost in the swarm
of anxious thoughts rattling my brain
It's so loud inside my head
I can't hear the world around me above the
roaring

Weapons

Thoughts are loud inside my head
Somedays I think of flowers and sunshine
others I think of hopelessness
I make a list of weapons to use
in the war inside my head
with coping skills and self-care
I prepare myself for battle
against the coming grey days

Wildflowers

Tiny purple flowers poke out of the sidewalk
growing where they want
forging a path in unfriendly conditions
Flowers of all colors and sizes
grow abundantly on the mountainside
basking in the sunlight
decorating the earth
sustaining the world by supporting the bees
growing beautiful and resilient
providing and decorating
bold and bright

Good Morning

Drip, drip, drip
coffee brews as the morning wakes
filling the house with its sweet aroma
I sit in the quiet
soaking in the peacefulness
as the sun shows her first rays of light over the
treetops
the birds and squirrels wake with me
the first sip reaches my lips
I savor the warmth
as the caffeine kick starts my brain
and the coffee refreshes my soul

Captivity

Birds falling
Down, down, down
To be whisked away by an unforgiving wind
And lost in the abyss.

Tears falling
Down, down, down
To be wiped away by an unforgiving sleeve
And lost in the abyss.

Pain pulling
Down, down, down
To drown the unforgiven victim:
She is lost in the captivity of her mind.

Mountains

I stand at the base of the mountain
looking up at the peak in the sky
14,000 feet high
I'm 5'2"
I hike higher and stare in awe
at the peak covered in crystal glaciers
glittering in the sunlight
contrasting against her bright blue backdrop
I feel the mountain under my feet as I hike
strong and steady
mesmerized by the beauty she holds
in the trees and flowers that grow on her
in the animals that live their life there
happily eating and breeding in their security
run-off from the glaciers creates beautiful lakes
Clear water glitters in the sunlight
I find a nice spot to sit
and have a snack
and marvel in the vastness of this world
and the smallness of me

Toxic positivity

live, laugh, love, good vibes only
But good cannot be felt without bad to contrast
Growth comes from the roots
in the dark under the dirt
while the flower blooms in the sunlight
the flower cannot bloom without the struggle
from the roots
in the dark under the dirt
good comes from perseverance and moments
in the dark under the dirt
reach through the dirt to find nutrients
absorb them to make the flower bold
but remember the work done
in the dark under the dirt

Taking Trauma

I take your trauma too
when I leave your home after a crisis
when I watch your family cry
when I hear your story

I take your trauma too
I feel it long after I leave you
My heart aches along yours
I mourn with you

I take your trauma too
It haunts my dreams
I spend my days researching ways to help
I want to take your pain

I take your trauma too
I come when you call
I cry on my drive home
I think about you at dinner

I take your trauma too
I will stay with you in the trenches
I will hand you a shovel and help you dig your
way out
You are not alone

Tranquility

Leaves dance in the wind
lake water ripples when tiny fish swim by
mockingbirds repeat the pretty songs they hear
squirrels race through trees
jumping from branch to branch
the sun shimmers through the leaves
decorating the forest floor in splashes of light
my mind is at peace
calm rushes over me like cool water on a hot day
I sit on the forest floor
and relish in the rarity of tranquility

www.ingramcontent.com/pod-product-compliance
Lightning Source LLC
La Vergne TN
LVHW021351200726
843509LV00014B/2788